Dogged Doggerel
AND OTHER
LITERARY DIVERSIONS

Dogged Doggerel
AND OTHER LITERARY DIVERSIONS

Charles Benton Manley

ST. LOUIS • 2015

Copyright © 2015 by Charles Benton Manley. All rights reserved.
No part of this book may be reproduced or distributed in any form or by any electronic or mechanical means, or stored in a database or retrieval system, without written permission of the copyright owner.

Printed in the United States of America

ISBN 978-0-692-56652-7

Some of these poems first appeared in the newsletter for the Washington University College of Arts and Sciences Lifelong Learning Institute, the newsletter for the Chess Club and Scholastic Center of Saint Louis, and the newsletter for the Dorchester Apartments. "In the Afternoon Light" was composed by Olivia Cook and Charles Manley as part of the Skipped Generation Project, a collaboration of the Washington University in St. Louis Writing Program and the Lifelong Learning Institute.

The dust jacket painting is by artist Jane Riley of Bath, England. Jane and her husband, George, have been good friends of the author's family for many years.

CONTENTS

Preface ~ ix

DOGGEREL

Kindness Now ~ 3
Perfecting the Golden Rule ~ 4
"Glad to Meet Cha" ~ 5
Barky Hierarchy ~ 6
Let Them Eat Baklava ~ 7
Screen Slavery ~ 8
What Matters ~ 9
Now Hear This! ~ 10
The Admonition of Adam and Eve ~ 11
Close, But No Cigarillo? ~ 12
No Time Like the Present ~ 13
Berkeleying Up the Wrong Tree ~ 14
Rearview Fear ~ 15
Bouquet for Today ~ 16
The Aged Existentialist ~ 17
My Misapprehension ~ 18
Dread Confusion ~ 19

POEMS

Yo, Too, Can Be a Clod ~ 23

To a Seed ~ 24

Nursery Crimes ~ 25

As I Head Down to the Laundry ~ 26

Gettysburg Prayer ~ 27

Welcome Ye to "Old" New Delhi ~ 28

Where Art Thou, Cart? ~ 30

Quietude ~ 32

In the Afternoon Light ~ 33

Bloom Where You're Planted ~ 34

To Try (Hymn) ~ 36

A Poem to K.J.P. on Her Birthday ~ 37

An Ode to Kimberly on Her 40th ~ 40

To Kimberly ~ 43

The Waif of St. Martha's Hall ~ 50

The Carousel of Life ~ 52

The Falls Church Address ~ 53

Shore Song ~ 54

A Perfect Marco Stay ~ 55

The Shuter Place ~ 56

High Wyoming Home ~ 58

The Door at 30 Portland Place ~ 59

For Tolly at Eighty ~ 63

CHESS PIECES

Connected Rooks ~ 67
What Do You Call a Whatchamacallit? ~ 68
Isolated "d," Please Not Me! ~ 69
Pawn Admonition ~ 70

ESSAYS

The Quiet Streets of Lower Pleasantville ~ 73
Affirmation ~ 79
To Make Believe ~ 81
Malthus: What Did He Say, And Does It Matter? ~ 85
"Cool" ~ 91
Stories My Father Told Me (I Think) and Selected
Short Subjects ~ 93

PREFACE

YOU MAY FIND IT CURIOUS that I label my poetic efforts *Dogged Doggerel*. Dictionaries define *doggerel* as "verse that is loosely styled and irregular in measure, especially for comic effect" or "poor or trivial verse." I feel quite differently. To me, my doggerel is like a favorite old dog with a bone. I'm very comfortable with him as he is.

I have a lifelong interest in writing poems: I wrote my first poem when I was 15 years old and in high school. "To a Seed" is included in this book, for better or for worse. Many of the early poems in this collection are limerick-like: four or five lines that usually rhyme, with a little kick at the end. The essays at the end of the book tend to be more serious, even sober. I think the poems reflect my best efforts.

I spent my entire medical career at Children's Hospital in St. Louis, employed by Washington University as a staff physician and retiring in 1994. I express my profound gratitude to the two people who helped me most: Marty Kraatz, my secretary, and Debbie Juhl, my nurse.

On the subject of memorable people, I wish to mention one other person: Hazel Flett, who taught ninth grade at Jarrett Junior High School in Springfield, Missouri. She was commonly called "Brutally Frank Flett" because she frequently used that phrase when correcting errant students. She would say, "Charles, I'm going to have to be brutally frank with you until you get it right." She was my very favorite teacher.

Several of my poems have been inspired by my three grown children, Ben, Bill, and Anne; my wife, Kimberly; and old and dear friends, including Charles Chalender, Bob Payne, and my many friends at First Unitarian Church of St. Louis.

CHARLES BENTON MANLEY
October 2015

Dogged Doggerel
AND OTHER
LITERARY DIVERSIONS

DOGGEREL

Kindness Now

The Future's somewhere up ahead,
We've left the past behind.
But for this moment in between,
It matters to be kind.

Perfecting the Golden Rule

An exception to the Golden Rule
That must not be dismissed:
"Do unto others" can't apply
If used by masochists.

"Glad to Meet Cha"

I always feel bad or should I say "badly,"
For people who don't suffer fools gladly.
It's bad enough that they don't feel glad
But even tougher in having to suffer.

Barky Hierarchy

Alpha dogs, Beta dogs
Running through the night.
Alphas often seem surprised
When Betas, on occasion, bark,
Or even, rarely, bite.

Let Them Eat Baklava

As far as I can see,
The best that I can tell,
It all looks good to me,
It all is going well.

Is there trouble up ahead?
No, really, not a chance.
And you can count on what I say,
'Cause I'm the King of France!

Screen Slavery

Smart kids, bright kids
Texting through the night.
But teachers aren't at all surprised
That they can't read or write.

What Matters

It matters to me what I believe.
It matters that what I believe, I say.
It matters that what I say, I do.
Beyond that, it really doesn't matter.

Now Hear This!

It's clear that *Here and Now*
 is not the same as *Now and Then*.
While *Here and There*'s most anywhere
 and doesn't deal with *When*.
So is the word *Hereafter*
 the same as *Evermore*?
I can't say, but when you leave,
 be sure you close the door.

The Admonition of Adam and Eve

The Lord told them to propagate,
They took him at his word.
But twelve billion progeny
Is really quite absurd.

Close, But No Cigarillo?

It's really nice to be precise,
But matter of fact, so is exact.
The difference isn't very great:
They're very nearly approximate.

No Time Like the Present

DEDICATED TO THE MEMORY OF DELARIVIER MANLEY,
THE FEMALE PLAYWRIGHT WHO IN 1696 COINED
THE PHRASE "THERE'S NO TIME LIKE THE PRESENT"

There's no time like the present,
No present like more time.
"Buddy, can you spare a moment?"
"Sorry, I use all of mine."

Berkeleying Up the Wrong Tree

A tree fell in the forest,
No one was around.
The question now before us:
Did it make a sound?

Profound the thought, it didn't,
But since no one was there
To hear a sound that wasn't,
Does anybody care?

Rearview Fear

You ask what is it most I fear
And I reply both loud and clear:
"The mirrored objects that I see
Are closer than appear to be."
Oh, dear! Oh, me!

Bouquet for Today

The bloom is fading from my face,
My stem has started tilting.
But for today, I'll grace this vase,
Tomorrow's time for wilting.

The Aged Existentialist

"Who am I?
Where am I?
What am I doing here?"

A mantra I find useful
To keep my thinking clear.
But now I say it every day
Instead of once a year!

My Misapprehension

Things are seldom what they seem,
Life is nothing but a dream.
Which makes me wonder who we are,
And where the hell I parked my car.

Dread Confusion

I wonder where I put my hat?
I really don't know where it's at.
I guess I'll wear my cap instead,
Why, here's my hat right on my head.

Well, now I wonder where's my cap?
I had it when I took my nap.
It may have fallen off the bed
Or may be underneath the spread.

I searched the bed, it wasn't there,
And I can't find it anywhere.
A burning doubt fills me with dread:
I wonder where I put my head?

POEMS

Yo, Too, Can Be a Clod

WITH APOLOGIES TO WILLIAM WORDSWORTH

I wandered lonely as a clod,
Bt thoght it was distinctly odd.
While I was low down pon the grond,
My friends were p high in the sky.
Bt then I fond the reason why,
I'd qite forgot the letter "u."
As soon as "u" was re-inserted,
I soared high, now undeserted,
While my heart with pleasure fills
To view the jocund daffodils.

To a Seed

HIGH SCHOOL, 1951

My backyard is the whole wide world,
And on its crowded, fertile plain,
Small seeds from everywhere are hurled,
Now waiting for the coming rain.

But when they're small, they're much the same,
You can't compare them, seed to seed,
That this one's from a chrysanthemum,
That one's from a thistle weed.

But most of them are seeds of grass,
And though they're neither great nor tall,
So when the oak tree dies at last,
They'll be the ones to break the fall!

Nursery Crimes

"Jack and Jill went up the hill to fetch a pail of water."

Now, if you believe that, I've got a bridge for sale in Brooklyn that's a real bargain. No, they don't put wells at the top of hills, they put them at the bottom. Water runs downhill, for Chrissake. If you want some water, you go to a 7-Eleven and get a bottle of Fiji or Natural Springs, raspberry-flavored. No, Jack and Jill didn't climb no hill, they got a bottle of booze and went to bed.

"Jack fell down and broke his crown, and Jill came tumbling after."

The truth is, Jack got frisky from all that whiskey, fell out of bed, and hit his head upon the floor. Jill, consumed with laughter, tumbled after. The moral of this story is, and there ain't much, Don't go telling stories 'bout climbing hills with leaky buckets that don't hold water!

As I Head Down to the Laundry
WITH APPRECIATION TO KEN DODDS

As I head down to the laundry,
How do I believe, How do I believe,
The very same washer that makes my clothes clean
Can gobble my socks up, just to be mean?

Sweet is, sweet the gurgle, sweet the gurgle,
And the hum, the hum of the Whirlpool, the Whirlpool.
I close my eyes and the world disappears,
But the heady perfume, the heady perfume
Of Tide's "Summer Breeze" remains.

So onward upstairs, my clothes now dry,
And only to sort and to fold.
But I know sometime later I'll return again
To search for one sock, brown and gold.

Gettysburg Prayer

His voice was high and reedy-thin,
His speech was over ere begun.
Not many heard his words that day,
And yet he kept our nation one.

Oh, Abe, if you're out there somewhere,
And you can hear my prayer somehow,
They really needed you back then,
Oh, Abe, we really need you now.

Welcome Ye to "Old" New Delhi
A PARODY OF RESPECT AND APPRECIATION FOR THE POETRY OF SIR RUDYARD KIPLING

Once ye nestled west of Bowery
Where Mulberry-Bleecker meets,
And ye sidled down the sidewalks
Of yer ol' Manhattan streets.

But the temple bells were callin'
And it's there that you would be,
By the ol' Moulmein Pagoda
Lookin' lazy at the sea.

For the wind is in the palm trees
And the temple bells, they say:
"Come ye *east*, ye New York Yankees,
Come ye *east* to Mandalay."

Now you're somewhere east of Suez
Buzzin' busy as the bees,
And ye got no time for lollin'
'Round resplendent embassies.

So as Vicki is exploring
In untrammeled cognate lobes,
So are Ben and Rhys a-rollin'
Down some tuk-tuk ridden roads.

Yet there should be time for leapin'
As the Flyin' Fishes do,
But with lots of learnin' certain
And explorin' Indie too.

So go hoppin' 'bout New Delhi
Like the bobbin' of a cork,
And before you even know it,
You'll be back in Ol' New York!

Where Art Thou, Cart?
POSTED NOTICE IN ELEVATORS

To all who in Dorchester dwell
Our greetings, may we wish you well.
We know you're of kind heart and true
And always try the right to do.
Therefore we hope you'll do your part
And Please Return Your Grocery Cart.

For sure, it's hard when at day's end,
And you've had gridlocks to contend
And crowded aisles and lines to best,
Now at last you've reached your nest.
But just before you shut your door,
Remember that you've one more chore.

The emptied cart, its purpose through,
Is wanted now by others too,
And like Horatius-at-the-Gate
Return is better soon than late.
So back along the hall you creep
With yards to go before you sleep.

Seconds later, maybe greater,
Put it on the elevator.
Return it to the lobby floor,
We will thank you even more.
And if returned to room for vending,
Sainthood application pending.

So do to others as to you,
Your good deed will help you too.
The reward, like Virtue, heeded.
You'll have a cart whenever needed.
Best of all, there'll be no need
To send you screed like this to read.

Quietude

One snowy winter's evening long ago,
Ralph Waldo Emerson and Henry David Thoreau
sat before the fire and watched the embers
slowly fade and die. Then Thoreau arose
and spoke for the first time:
"A most pleasant evening, Emerson,"
to which a silent nod was made.
Thoreau put on his coat and exited
through the door into the night.

One quiet summer's afternoon, not long ago,
I (Homo sapiens) and a fly (Musca domestica)
sat and watched transforming clouds as they slowly
moved across the sky. At sunset, the fly twitched
his forelegs together twice, flew a dipterous circle
about my head, and was gone. I know
we both had a most pleasant time.

In the Afternoon Light

SKIPPED GENERATION POETRY
BY OLIVIA COOK AND CHARLES MANLEY

What are you waiting for, for instance, and is the bus
the working men ride in the coincidence of your life?
You would take it anywhere
from the skyscraper that splits the street in two

from the skyscraper that splits the street in two
We're riding by it in the midst of New York City.
"I found myself agape, admiring the prow of the Flatiron Building
in the afternoon light."

in the afternoon light
the city is anyone's reality, faint recognizable trait,
the city is the transformable body
the sidewalks widen to accommodate.

the sidewalks widen to accommodate
Like a network of interlacing
strength, serenity, and nearness.
It is a neighborhood, not a jungle.

It is a neighborhood, not a jungle.
Crowds shuffle along from one newsstand to the next
at the corner of Here, and a too familiar There,
but there you are, stilled.

But there you are, stilled
With Broadway on one side and the opening
Of Madison Square on the other,
The wind currents against the Flatiron are treacherous.

Bloom Where You're Planted

So what is this life all about?
You get no say in where you sprout.
You send down roots where'er you be
And shoot up chlorophyllically.
Buds pop out in wild profusion,
Awkward, generative confusion.
All of a sudden, much too soon
You blossom forth in glorious bloom.

Some get chosen for the vase,
Others waste in desert space.
Regardless, you know what they say:
"Every flower has its day."
Slowly, you begin to fade
And find that you prefer the shade.
Time has its way, you wilt and shrink
And finally get tossed in the sink.

But would you have another way?
No way, José, not for a day.
Plastic flower—not an hour!
Live forever—no, not never!
On other hand, Life's often grand
And better than if it was planned.
For example, you get cut
And with a bunch in vase you're stuck.
But maybe better than you think:
For one, you get all you can drink!

And if you smile and do your duty
You may get placed next to a cutie.
In any case, make of it best
And then, in time, you'll find your rest
And maybe learn why you were granted
"To Bloom Wherever You Are Planted"!

To Try (Hymn)*

Now, *greet the morning light with* brave intent.
Hammer the golden day until it lies
A glimmering plate to heap with memory;
Salute arriving moments with your eyes.

We live, we are elected Now by time
Few out of many not yet come to *be*
And many *others who have gone before*
Our time, our place, our own Eternity

So break the silence with a voice *upraised,*
Until the shades of evening claim the sky,
Press mind and body hard against this world
And Peace shall come to those who dared to Try.

*New words for Hymn No. 178, "Now Give Heart's Onward Habit Brave Intent," in the old blue Unitarian hymnal (*Hymns for the Celebration of Life*, 1964).

A Poem to K.J.P. on Her Birthday

Sing Ho to my Kimberly Jean,
She's the neatest thing I've ever seen.
She's bright and she's purty,
And now she is thirty,
In her bones, not a streak is there mean.

From her roots in the hills of PA,
She grew up in Falls Church, VA.
With sibs Ann and Joan,
Like weeds were they grown,
Tall, red-haired, and plenty to say.

Unitarian, Kim was from the start,
As their first nun, she thought t'would be smart.
Then she found that for fun,
They really had none.
Am I glad that she had change of heart.

Off to Vassar, she sought perfection
In an environmental direction.
But it was in Poughkeepsie,
That she first got tipsy
Learning more about natural selection.

After more degrees did she go
Out west to the land of MO.
And to this day,
That's where she's stayed,
And the rest, you pretty much know.

How at Monsanto, their research she audits,
From her crew she receives many plaudits.
But she does cause some rages
When she rattles their cages
And their data don't look like it oughta.

Though possessing a city-girl charm,
She also spends time on the farm.
Checking cows in the stable,
She's really quite able
To make sure they come to no harm.

I first met Kim in the choir.
Her singing, I soon did admire.
Drawn in spirit's tether,
We then sang together.
Now our duet goes higher and higher.

Though you might not think she's that sort,
She's really a very good sport.
Be it golfing or biking,
Aerobics or hiking,
Though broomball is really her forte.

Though it's said that she knows where she's spent
Each and every dime, nickel, and cent,
I think that it's nifty,
That she is so thrifty,
On my wallet it makes less a dent.

As a person, she's tried and true.
When in need, she always comes through.
Best of all, don't you see,
  She puts up with me,
Which is something that's quite hard to do.

So here's to my Kimberly P.,
Whose years now number thirty.
Though she's come a long way
From Falls Church, VA,
The best's yet to come, wait and see.

An Ode to Kimberly on Her 40th

Listen my friends and you shall hear
Of the wondrous life of Kimberly dear.
'Twas the 8th of March in '55
That she did first come alive
And all the heavens did clap and cheer.

In the Keystone State, Meadville, PA,
Kimberly Jean first saw her way
To father Bob and Nancy mom.
What matter if she sucked her thumb,
By all accounts, she made their day.

The Perry sisters numbered three,
They were, and are, a sight to see.
With older Ann and younger Joan,
Kimberly is a middle-grown,
Perhaps why she's so agreeably.

To Hamilton, O for a short while,
But Falls Church, VA was more their style,
Where she was found of good opinion
And flourished in the "Old Dominion,"
On every face she made a smile.

Then in pursuit of higher knowledge,
She headed off to Vassar College.
A lot to learn in Poughkeepsie,
How to avoid getting too tipsy,
And the Mazola Oil parties that were alleged.

Dad Perry is an engineer
And so became his daughters dear.
Kimberly had said, "What the heck,"
Then headed off to old Virginia Tech
And there she stayed for several year.

And then she thought "I think it's best
To get a job," and headed west.
When she saw the Arch, it made her smile.
She said, "I'll stay here for a while."
Perhaps you know about the rest.

Being environmentally concerned
At Monsanto, a place she's earned
With coveralls, boots, and old hard hat,
By many a sewer she has sat,
And oh the regs that she has learned.

Although not a contrarian,
And though its rather rare of one
Free of any kind of malice,
A daughter of the flaming chalice,
She's a natural-born Unitarian.

To First Church she came and joined the choir
To sing the parts both high and higher.
'Twas here upon the scene I came,
To get to know her was my aim,
More than her voice did I admire.

With time, our feelings grew to be
Such did she cast her lot with me.
'Twas in the fall of '87
That we were joined in blissful heaven
With Earl of Holt as referee.

Since then, the years have flown right by
So fast, you have to wonder why.
By bike, on foot, alone, en masse,
We've explored many a far trail or pass
From Rodney Stoke to Telluride.

So, here's to my dear Kimberly.
Who would believe that she's forty?
With all the good times we have known
And all the good friends we have grown,
There's many more good times to be.

To Kimberly

UPON CELEBRATION OF FIFTY YEARS OF LIFE
8 MARCH 1955

I

As one may teach when least aware,
So many may your virtues be.
There is so much for you to share,
Loved by so many, just like me.

My grandkids three, when here in town,
Sometimes we take them to the zoo.
From work, you're gridlocked, homeward bound
And they arrive before you do.

"Where's Kim-Kim?" "She'll be here soon."
"Is Kim-Kim going to the zoo?"
"Oh yes, she's going." "Where's she at?"
"She won't be long." (I hope it's true!)

Then, a key sounds in the lock,
You are opening the door.
"Kim-Kim!" rushing, greeting, hugging,
Order is once more restored.

When they've brought a present for you
Or some other such surprise,
I can hear it in their voices,
I can see it in their eyes.

"I made it just for you today!"
"How nice, but what's it supposed to be?"
"Well, do you like it?" "Yes, I love it."
Then, a vindicated "SEE!"

Kimberly has a pair of sisters,
She's the sister-in-between.
The three together constitute
A perfect sibling trilogy.

To me, what's most remarkable,
Indeed, may well be unique:
All three of them are engineers,
An extraordinary feat.

The cause of this career congruence
Soon becomes quite crystal clear:
They followed footsteps of their father,
The prototypic engineer.

For this achievement to occur
Required a virtuosa's eye.
Their mother guiding through the years
While making perfect pecan pie.

Now the sisters, all together,
Photo taken on the beach,
I see a camaraderie
That speaks of love without a speech.

Both benevolent brothers-in-law,
Nifty nephews, frisky niece.
An avuncular aunt and uncle
Sending their love sans cesse.

We had our share, wide-open spaces,
Drove the "Road Towards the Sun."
From my kids, the love is there.
With Kimberly, we are as one.

When, at first, she went to work
For her chemical company,
They soon learned she got things done.
Leave her alone and done they'd be.

With resolve downright Churchillian,
Some say, sometimes, stubbornness.
She is the best that she can be
But plays her cards close to the vest.

Both her boss and secretary,
On the basis of this hunch,
Now stay far out of her way
Except when they go out to lunch.

II

Drop a pebble in a pond,
Watch the ripples spread beyond.
Circles growing ever wider
Going on and on and on.

My crew of two for 30 years
Both headed south when time was up,
Long since were Kim's cheerleaders.
(Who do you think typed this up?)

My teenage best friend, C.H.C.,
Later both ways "best men" be.
C. and P. good friends to Kim,
As I know they'll always be.

And the friends I've yet to mention
From her new activity:
Area Alumna President,
Vassar College, Poughkeepsie.

Old-time friends from long ago,
Scattered where the four winds blow.
Yet they go on corresponding
And will keep on doing so.

III

Congratulations, Kimberly,
You've lived a half a century!
That's 50 years, so Cheers, My Dear!
May you have that or more to be.

And half your life, hard to believe,
You've shared with me, dear friend and wife.
That's half a half a century.
They've been the best years of my life.

First, she was my e-mail sender,
Then, plenipotentiary.
Now, she's prime decision maker
And that's as it ought to be.

I love to hear the way you talk,
I love to listen to you sing.
I love to see the way you walk,
I love about you everything.

It all started with a song,
At First Church in the choir we sang,
And there we made our wedding vows
And still we sing on in refrain:

"My life flows on in endless song,
Above Earth's lamentations.
I hear the real, though far-off, hymn
That hails a new creation."

"Through all the tumult and the strife,
I hear the music ringing.
It sounds an echo in my soul.
How can I keep from singing?"

There, as elsewhere, you come through
You know your part, your pitch is true.
You're always in your place on time,
They know that they can count on you.

After practice, to Geno's house,
Dear old sommelier and host.
So many years, prime après choir,
Good wine, good times, good friends to toast.

IV

"Out on the street, out on the lot,
Don't miss a single little spot!"

Kimberly's favorite chore, no question.
Above all else, it is her thing.
Although it's not an obsession,
She's the Queen of Litter-pick-up-ing.

"Here today, tomorrow not,
Get the litter while it's hot!"

Her favorite present I ever gave her
Was her Litter-picker-upper.
Only better would have been
Two or three or more of them.

"All that's gold does not glitter.
Bend that back, don't be a quitter."

If she were to have a fault
(Although a fault it's really not)
Her love of getting litter and
When and where and how it's got.

"Ours is not to ponder 'STOP,'
Ours is pick up 'til we drop."

Of course, you know that I am kidding.
I'm a litter-picker-upper too,
And, in fact, more times than not
I constitute her entire crew.

V

Nonetheless, can't overstate,
She does so much from doing good,
And doing good brings many friends,
Too many to note, as I should.

With love from waif, St. Martha's Hall,
From sisters, uncle, brothers-in-law,
Mother, father, aunts galore,
In-laws, out-laws, who knows what-laws,

From choir and church, city, state,
"Our country 'Tis of thee," you're great.
Sun, moon, planets, and Milky Way,
A billion galaxies on the way.
Happy Fifty, Kim!

The Waif of St. Martha's Hall

A haven is St. Martha's Hall,
where inner-city kids can come
and, for a while, be safe from all
the dirty tricks that fate has sprung.

Among them is a little boy,
don't know his name, nor seen his face.
Yet I must know him just as well
as if I were there in his place.

When you're there, too, to lend a hand,
upon your lap he wants to be,
His favored thumb stuck in his mouth,
"serene as Buddha 'neath his tree."

Safe from all "fell circumstance,"
still as a statue but his eyes,
he notes his opportunities
while waiting for his nerve to rise.

Suddenly he's off and gone,
the therapeutic thumb full spent.
He flies to join the playroom throng,
his countenance now confident.

Running, tumbling, shrieking, jumping,
giving just as good as gets,
climbing, riding, swinging, sliding,
fair and foul, with no regrets.

But now and then, a furtive glance
to relocate your whereabouts,
and thus avoid the awful chance
of no escape to his redoubt.

He knows that he can range afar,
yet not so far the route retrace,
a quick retreat to where you are,
his certain, safe, and kindly place.

Now's the time with Kindness in it.
Here's the place with Grace for all.
As once there was in time and space
for this waif, St. Martha's Hall.

The Carousel of Life

TO KIMBERLY, ON HER SIXTIETH BIRTHDAY

We're riding on a merry-go-round, the Carousel of Life.
We don't remember getting on, or just how long the ride has been.
The only thing we know, for sure, is that, in time, our ride will end.

But as for now, the moon is high, and you are standing by my side.
The organ makes a rumbling beat, the calliope plays a sprightly
    song,
  and we go riding round and round and on and on and on.

We're not alone on our Ride of Life. Sturdy steeds go galloping by
with frozen faces and soulless eyes. Grenadier guards stand tall
    and straight,
  just as they did at Buckingham Gate.

I see the starlight in your eyes,
  Your hair is ruffled by the breeze.
You are my love, my wife, the true companion of my life,
  as we go riding onward through the night.

The Falls Church Address

Two score and ten years ago, our father and mother together brought forth on this continent a new family, conceived in Meadville and dedicated to the proposition that we would be well loved, well fed, and have a week at the beach every summer.

Now we are met at 4207 23rd Street, Arlington, Virginia 22207 to commemorate this exceptional union of fifty dedicated years. It is altogether fitting and proper that we should do this, considering all the money they blew on us.

But in a larger sense, we cannot dedicate, we cannot consecrate, we cannot hallow this ground, because they live at 814 Villa Ridge Road, Falls Church, Virginia 22046.

The world will little note nor long remember what we say here, and Thank God for that. It is rather for us to take increased devotion to the union of Bob Perry and Nancy Maurer—that we here highly resolve that they shall not have changed diapers in vain but that we, the offspring, as well as spouses, grandchildren, relatives, friends, and hangers-on, do hereby honor, love, and cherish this wonderful couple and their fifty years together.

    KIMBERLY AND CHARLES
    June 10, 2001

Shore Song

Sand, sea, sky, sunrise seaward, shore strolling, sauntering, striding. Soaring seagulls, scampering sandpipers, scurrying sand crabs, salty sea air, surf sounds, seaweed, sand dunes, soothing sea breeze, sea shells.

Swan Street sanctuary, set-out, shredded wheat, sweet rolls, skim milk, strawberries, self-serve, sit around soft sofas, story scanning, short-word spelling skill, schachspiel study. Summer selection sentence sequence sighting* (sorry), snapshots, stories. Synergy.

Sun summit, starving stomachs, some scarfing smoothies, salad, Swiss-salami sandwiches, Samuel Adams. Supine siesta, sleeping, snoring, snoozing; showering, swimming suits, shore, sand, sea-swelling surf, sandals, sunglasses, sunblock, sunburn.

Sun sliding: sipping signal. Sommelier selected Sauvignon, Shiraz, some spirits, scotch, soda. Sunset, scrumptious, savory suppers, shrimp, spaghetti, sweet corn, squash soufflé, salut, santé, Satiety.

Swapping supper-table stories, side-splitting sketchtionery sessions, stumpers, spouting, shouting. Supreme star Sirius; Sagan, satellites, simmering, steaming sauna, soaking, soothing, soundly slumber.

Seven suns swiftly set, sea to shining sea, someplace, sometime, Serenity!

---

*Summer vacation book reading.

A Perfect Marco Stay
SUNG TO "WITH SOMEONE LIKE YOU"

With dear wife, Kim, my pal thick or thin,
We got to leave it all behind, and go unwind.
How could we know the Shuters' condo
Is best there is south of Orlando?

We found perfect peace, down in the Southeast,
Up high beneath a clear blue sky.
No storms, no rain, no hurricane,
Many thanks to Renni and Eli.

The Shuter Place
VISITS TO A FRIEND'S CONDOMINIUM IN FLORIDA

Would you believe, like kith and kin,
The Manley Clan is back again.

To Shuters' aerie in the sky,
We want our very best to try

To be behaved, and yet have fun,
At Marco Island in the sun.

It seems like only yesterday
When first we came awhile to stay.

I know that we've been here times four,
Or maybe five, or even more.

And all the while we've learned the place
And we are almost known by face.

The gulls and terns out on the shore
Don't seem so skittish as before.

The gators welcome us with smiles
As we're air-boating mangrove isles.

The Shuters' nest we know by heart,
Each nook and cranny well apart.

A favorite sock, of gold and brown,
This year within the laundry room was found.

Their liquor cabinet we esteem
Is graced by our old friend, Jim Beam.

The sand we've scattered on the floor,
The keys we've lost to their front door.

So what's the point? It's simply this:
We LOVE this place of peace and bliss.

No, we'll not make no claims or fights,
But, ain't we got some SQUATTER'S RIGHTS?

High Wyoming Home

Oh, give me a home where the grizzly bears roam
And the deer and the antelope play.
But we'd rather be there, with Stanley and Claire,
Than anywhere else we can say!

High Wyoming Home,
Where the Birges are "being" all day.
It truly is a heaven on earth.
Our thanks for a wonderful stay.

The Door at 30 Portland Place

I've never thought about *doors* a lot,
They are objects that swing open and shut.
I assumed that doors were all the same,
But they're not!

One of my very most favorite doors
is the door of the house where the Leonards live.
My affection has nothing to do with its looks:
That's not it!

True, it's attractive and Esley, if asked,
Might say it was "nice," but lacked any "passion."
The reason for my rapport with their door is:
We're old friends!

On many occasions, for many a year
I have been blessed to pass through its portals
To a favorite place on the face of the earth:
Geno's house!

Often when I'm coming up the front walk,
I detect a faint smile on the face of the door.
Some say it's a crease, or a crack in the paint:
No, it ain't.

When I open the door, it may make a faint creak
As if to welcome me back, so to speak.
You may think it's strange that I feel this way,
And it is!

As I close the door, the knob gets a squeeze
To reciprocate that I'm glad to be back,
Back with my friends on Portland Place
Once again!

For many a year, I've been visiting there
To participate on various occasions
That Geno would host
Throughout his house.

Begin with the east porch: balmy spring evenings,
Sipping, candlelight, swing set to swinging.
Into the night, a dozen of those,
I suppose.

One night, starlight started us singing,
An old refrain that we knew by heart.
While neighbors most likely were praying for rain
Even worse.

Then, standing around the dining room table,
Birthdays, holidays, wedding receptions,
Some participants laughing a lot,
Others not!

Celebrants trying savory canapés,
Champagne exquisite, with fine bubbles streaming,
Geno and Connie, smiling and gracious,
Welcoming faces!

The living room, best on cold winter nights
In front of the fire, a place of delights.
And to give it grace
A "fireplace face."

The kitchen's culinary central command,
The place to be for any gourmand,
Telling his stories, talking nonstop
Till popcorn pops!

Geno's a connoisseur, no doubt of that,
An epicure, oenophile, it is a fact.
But the one thing he savors more than wine:
Other people.

It's true about Leonard,
He's not Walter Mitty.
His guffaw can carry as far as Wright City,
And break glass.

But most of all, and through it all, the grace
And welcome in his face. And all
The while, behind the smile, courage enough for
All of us.

The last time we exited his front door
And down the walk into the night,
The smile was back just as before,
To me, a most heartwarming sight.

So in reply, I stopped to say:
"Merci, porte d'entrée,
Et vous, Geno, merci beaucoup,
NOTRE TRÈS CHER GRAND SOMMELIER!"

For Tolly at Eighty

What does it mean whenever they say
That you are, as ever, as sharp as a tack?
Does it mean that your wardrobe is not off the rack?
That you like to eat cheddar that wants to bite back?
That your repartee, on occasion, may sting?
That you may be off-key sometimes when you sing?

"Mais non, that's not it," sez Hercule Poirot.
"It's your little grey cells that make you so."
And that being it, we want to say:

Have a happy birthday to celebrate being.

To help make certain you stay so keen,
Here are more sharp tacks for you, by golly,
So you will remain as

Sharp as a Tolly!

Chess has been a source of good fellowship among old friends,
including artist Stan Veyhl, who created this watercolor.
I have sat for many a long hour in front of the chess board
with Stan and another friend, Tom Archer.
Chess has also been the source of the poems that follow.

Connected Rooks

FOR KIMBERLY

The Rooks begin the game apart,
In latent state abide,
But, when connected, are enhanced
And dance both far and wide.

What Do You Call a Whatchamacallit?

There seems to be no unanimity of opinion about what we call those objects we push around a chess board. My suggestion is: What Do you Call a Whatchamacallit?

I know what you call a "piece,"
I know what you call a "pawn,"
But what do you call them both together
When both are called upon?

It's okay to say they're all pieces
When scattered about in a drawer.
But on display in the "array"?
Equality no more!

Some say they're "material,"
Others like "units" or "force."
There was a time they were "chessmen,"
Long ago, of course.

Among the chessmen is a "Queen,"
Most powerful but "gay"?
It's not too late to set things straight:
"Chess persons" all the way!

Isolated "d," Please Not Me!

I sent my "c" pawn out to play,
And just as I suspected,
Black took one look and "wham" he took:
Queen's Gambit pawn "Accepted."

Out came Black's "c" to trade my "e,"
Confirming all my fears.
My poor pawn "d," alone was he,
Away from all his peers.

"No reason for this gambit try,"
I'm feeling mighty low,
When suddenly, my rooks fly by,
Down open "c" they go.

The rest was "history," they say,
Black's King was soon checkmated.
The lesson then: At times, to win,
Some pawns must be ill-fated.

Pawn Admonition

See the slowly moving pawn,
No big leaps to count upon.
If he tries to move ahead
Of his fellow pawns, he's dead.
So as not to get exposed,
Pawns should remain juxtaposed.

ESSAYS

The Quiet Streets of Lower Pleasantville
2009

I

I AM A RETIRED PHYSICIAN, 76 years old, with Parkinson's disease. Almost every morning, I take my constitutional walk along the nearby streets of my apartment building, the Dorchester, in a residential area designated by Bill McClellan, columnist for the *St. Louis Post-Dispatch,* as "Lower Pleasantville." My wife, Kimberly, and I have been living at the Dorchester for more than 20 years. We enjoy the people who live and work there, the ambience, and the amenities.

This neighborhood is well known to history as the site of the 1904 St. Louis World's Fair, à la Judy Garland and "Meet Me in St. Louie, Louie, Meet Me at the Fair." The Dorchester actually occupies land where the Palace of Horticulture stood, and it is my understanding that the Filipino village was located on the site of present-day "Lower Pleasantville." It was rumored that the natives had a custom of eating dogs, thus naming the locality just to the south "Dogtown."

Lower Pleasantville (hereafter often designated "L.P.") is bounded on the east by Skinker Boulevard, a heavily traveled thoroughfare, and beyond that, by the leafy expanse of Forest Park, the second-largest municipal park in the nation and the principal site of the fair. The park contains several museums, golf courses, a zoo, and an area of primeval forest, among its many attractions.

To the south, Clayton Road is another broad and busy limit to L.P. The campus of Concordia Lutheran Seminary borders the west side, while to the north, the realm of Upper Pleasantville (U.P.), as designated by McClellan, extends to the hilltop campus of Washington

University in St. Louis. The homes in this locale are more substantial than in L.P. However, I find the latter to be much more interesting. In any case, while there is a sidewalk on DeMun connecting the two, there is no connecting street, so to drive an automobile from one to the other, you must exit and reenter via Skinker or Clayton.

Why, you may ask, is L.P. more interesting than U.P.? There are many reasons, but mainly three: the architecture, the kids, and the "downtown." About half of the buildings in L.P. are three-story red-brick apartments, some with unusual façades, such as faux balconies with balustrades and French windows. The other half are single-family houses, one and a half stories tall, each unique in appearance. This is where the kids are. All of these homes and apartments were constructed in the 1920s and '30s and are very well maintained. There are also five high-rise apartment and condo buildings, such as the Dorchester, grouped midway down Skinker at the junction of L.P. and U.P.

"Downtown" refers to the DeMun shopping district, which includes the contiguous sidewalk cafés of Shasta's Wine Bar, Jimmy's Restaurant, and Kaldi's Coffee Shop. There are also five or six storefront establishments, including a laundry, a hairdresser, and the Martial Arts School of Clayton. In good weather, the adjacent lawn of Concordia Seminary provides excellent space for sailing Frisbees or model airplanes, Tai Chi classes, and exercising dogs. At Northwood Street, just beyond Kaldi's, is the Captain School, the grade school for both L.P. and U.P. kids and, I understand, an excellent one.

As I mentioned, access to L.P. is limited. A small stone monument with the words *Hi-Pointe-DeMun* marks the entrance from Clayton Road. DeMun Avenue, with a grassy divider, winds down and disappears among the oak trees for a distance of four short blocks before reaching downtown. Besides this entrance, there are only three streets off Skinker and two off Clayton by which access can be made to L.P., three of the five being one-way.

The designation Hi-Pointe-DeMun indicates a topographical feature of the entrance: Hi-Pointe is named for its natural elevation above the rest of the City of St. Louis in all directions. Therein, I had a question for Bill McClellan: Lower Pleasantville is actually higher on the slope of Mount Hi-Pointe than Upper Pleasantville. Shouldn't the names be reversed?

Whatever the name, here—in the midst of a large metropolitan area of several million people extending to distant suburbs in all directions—lies a community that one is never likely to enter by chance, a sort of "Brigadoon" that is a perfect place to take a walk.

II

BY THE TIME I GET ORGANIZED in the morning, it's 10:30 or so. I have a standard route that I take for my constitutional. As I head out the front door of the Dorchester, there is usually a line of cars waiting for the prolonged stoplight at Rosebury. I pass in front of them and head up Skinker one block to Southwood, passing the Versailles and Wiltshire high-rise condos along the way. At Southwood, I turn right and enter Lower Pleasantville, walking west toward DeMun.

About 250 feet on Southwood, there was a bicycle chained to a light fixture, unmoved for as long as I had been walking this route. The bike appeared functional, although well used. I imagined all kinds of circumstances to explain this phenomenon. The owner was undoubtedly a student. Perhaps he or she had gone off to Europe or Boston or some other place of higher learning for a sabbatical in ethnography, ethnology, ethology, or even etymology, and figures that the weather had done as much harm to the bike as it could. One day when I came by, the bicycle was gone, lock and all, but on the next day, it was back again in its accustomed place. Order in the universe has been restored!

As I reach the summit of the hill, the sound of traffic on Skinker dies away. As I approach DeMun, I pass a magnolia and a dogwood, both resplendent in the springtime before our variable weather gets to them. The predominant tree in the Midwest is, of course, the oak, to which the many squirrels will happily attest. Maples also do well in L.P., complemented by a few gum and sycamore trees.

By mid-morning, the students have all gone to class or the library or Kaldi's with their laptop computers, so I am pretty much alone. In late summer and early fall, the only sound I often hear is that of crickets. An occasional automobile travels along Southwood, or an airliner may arch overhead. Workmen of various sorts are encountered: tuckpointers, tree trimmers, and UPS deliverymen, all preoccupied with their tasks. I can count on the fingers of one hand the times I have met a fellow perambulator, with at most a momentary eye contact, a smile, or a "good morning."

As I approach DeMun, the toddler's playground is on my right, surrounded by a tall, black, wrought-iron fence. The children are usually there in all kinds of weather, with their mothers standing about discussing the various issues of the day while keeping a watchful eye on the kids. The toddlers do what they do best: toddling, while emitting high-pitched sounds of exultation, punctuated by occasional outbursts of disputatious displeasure that require maternal adjudication.

At DeMun, I turn left and follow the curving sidewalk up to San Bonita Avenue, passing—guess what!—the home of the "king of Lower Pleasantville," Bill McClellan! One Sunday afternoon, I was taking a time-aberrant walk, when out of his house came Bill, preceded by two miniature bulldogs, each the size of a large bratwurst. Not yet leashed, they perceived me as hostile. Rushing over to contain them, he hollered, "Don't worry, they won't bite much."

As he got them leashed, I saw my opportunity, and took it: "Bill, I have a question I've been wondering about for some time."

"Shoot," he said.

"Is the name supposed to be 'Lower' or 'Lesser,' and does it matter?"

"It definitely matters, and it's 'Lower,' " he replied.

"Okay," I said, "and since that area down there (I pointed in the direction of Washington University) is definitely lower in elevation, shouldn't it be called 'Lower' and this 'Upper'?"

"No," he replied. "It doesn't have anything to do with topography. They're the 'Uppers,' and we're the 'Lowers,' and that's just the way it is." With that, he smiled, and with a tip of his cap, he was off in the direction of Concordia Seminary to exercise his two little yappers.

Continuing up San Bonita, I enter the heart of Munchkin Land, with its bungalows uniform in size and position, and yet each different from the last. The telltale hopscotch markings drawn on the sidewalk, along with an occasional scooter lying in a front yard, give a distinctive cachet to the surroundings. Yet there is virtually no litter to be seen, except for acorns.

Near the top of the hill, where Buena Vista Avenue begins and curves around to meet Alamo Avenue, I often rouse a dog within a house as I pass on the sidewalk, attesting to the acuity of his hearing and the infrequency with which he is disturbed. Apparently, the crickets, the occasional airliner passing overhead, and the acorns dropping on the pavement are within his screen of acceptable sounds.

My wife and I regularly take creative walks into the park or down into Upper, but for my constitutional, nothing beats the familiarity of my Lower route. Over time, I have come to know each chink or irregularity in the sidewalk pavement, for instance, the spot where the root of an oak tree has heaved the concrete slab into the shape of prayerful hands.

As I approach Skinker, I hear the sound of traffic again and retrace my steps down, past 801 (an all-glass high-rise), Southwood Street, the Wiltshire, the Versailles, and Rosebury Street to home base, the

Dorchester. My pedometer tells me that I have walked half a mile and it has taken me 17 minutes.

I know there are innumerable "Pleasantvilles" throughout St. Louis, the United States, and the world, but whether you call it "Lower" or "Upper," this is mine (and Bill McClellan's, of course), and my, it is indeed most "pleasant"!

Affirmation

PRESENTED AT FIRST UNITARIAN CHURCH, MARCH 31, 1985

THERE ARE FEW SUBJECTS that arouse more emotion among Unitarians than the relative merit of various hymns. One of my favorite hymns became so only recently, likely because I had been put off by its intimidating title and first line, "Now give heart's onward habit brave intent." Perhaps you would like to hear that again. "**Now** give heart's onward **habit** brave intent." Right. Fortunately, it gets better from there: "Hammer the golden day until it lies a glimmering plate to heap with memory. Salute arriving moments with your eyes."

Blaise Pascal, an early forerunner of existentialism, wrote, "When I consider the short duration of my life, swallowed up in the eternity before and after, the little space I fill, and even can see, engulfed in the infinite immensity of space of which I am ignorant and which knows me not, I am frightened and am astonished at being here rather than there, why now rather than then?"

The second verse of the hymn replies, "We live, we are elected now by time, few out of many not yet come to birth, and many dead, to use the daylight now, to stand beneath the sun upon the earth."

You may recall that in the play *Our Town* by Thornton Wilder, Emily has returned from the grave to the scenes of her childhood, but now it's time to go back and she says, "Goodbye, goodbye, world. Goodbye, Grover's Corners ... Mama and Papa. Goodbye to clocks ticking ... and Mama's sunflowers, and food and coffee, and new-ironed dresses and hot baths ... and sleeping and waking up. Oh, earth, you're too wonderful for anybody to realize you." And then she asks, "Do any human beings ever realize life while they live it—every, every minute?" And the answer she gets is "No... Well, the saints and poets, maybe they do some."

The last line of the hymn goes, "Then break the silence with a voice of praise, before we fall asleep, before we die, press mind and body hard against this world. Open the door that opens toward the skies."

Hammer the golden day, **break** the silence, **press** mind and body hard.... Yes, Emily, and some of the rest of us are trying, as well.

To Make Believe
2011

IN 1897, EIGHT-YEAR-OLD Virginia O'Hanlon wrote to the *New York Sun*. "Sir, please tell me the truth, is there a Santa Claus?"

In reply, an editorial by Francis Pharcellus Church said, "Yes, Virginia, there is a Santa Claus ... Thank God, he lives, and he lives forever. A thousand years from now, Virginia, nay, ten times ten thousand years from now, he will continue to make glad the heart of childhood."

One may ask, What does this have to do with the question "How do I think American Childhood has and hasn't changed since the 1840s?"

There's no question that it's changed, just as America has changed. There have been a thousand, nay, ten times ten thousand ways that American Childhood has changed since Samuel Clemens (Mark Twain) played on the banks of the Mississippi at Hannibal, Missouri. His recollections provided the basis for *The Adventures of Tom Sawyer* and other well-known stories.

The most important change from those antebellum days was, without a doubt, the Thirteenth Amendment to the Constitution, prohibiting slavery. A major change was the consequence of the industrial-technological revolution, which began in the early 1800s and continues to the present day. A significant effect, in addition to development of such things as the flush toilet, the electric light, the hydrogen bomb, and the paper clip, was the mass migration that occurred following the creation of, first steam, and then internal combustion engines.

In 1845, the population of St. Louis (just downstream from Hannibal) was about 70,000 people. By the end of the nineteenth century, it had risen to more than half a million and St. Louis was the fourth largest city in the United States. This is where Mark Twain got his pen name, from piloting steamboats up and down the Mississippi River.

But what about the ways in which American Childhood hasn't changed, and will never change? Examples that come to mind are a mother's love of her child, human nature, and memories of childhood's favorite things, such as "raindrops on roses and whiskers on kittens" (Oscar Hammerstein, *The Sound of Music*, 1959).

Recalling Hammerstein and another of his 945 lyrics, this one from the musical *Showboat* (1927): "We can make believe I love you, only make believe that you love me. Others find peace of mind in pretending. Couldn't you, couldn't I, couldn't we?"

It is human nature to pretend. We all do it. And in some instances, such as Santa Claus and "love at first sight," to make believe is probably harmless, so long as we recognize deep down that it's not reality. We can suspend disbelief for an hour or two and thereby get some pleasure in our lives with entertainment, for example, by going to the movies.

The danger comes when we start pretending too much. In 1932, the elected government of Germany made-believe that it could control Adolf Hitler—"outdo Machiavelli," they said. Instead, Hitler came within a cat's whisker of ending the world as we know it. Today, in 2011, we stand in equal danger or worse. I refer not to politics, military maneuvers, or evil dictators, but rather to the phenomenon of overpopulation.

It took more than *one million years* for the earth to reach a population of one billion people. This occurred by the early nineteenth century. Now, in 2011, the world contains nearly seven billion people; and twelve years from now, there will be a billion more! That's right, *twelve years* compared to *a million*; the rate of population growth is 80,000-plus times faster than it was in the prehistoric era!

Overpopulation is the nearly-seven-billion-pound gorilla sitting on the sofa in the living room that we quietly tiptoe around and pretend doesn't exist. What do we do about it? Make believe that the world will be alright for our children and grandchildren?

To Mark Twain is attributed the saying "Everyone talks about the weather, but no one does anything about it." I've adapted that saying for my purpose: "Almost no one talks about overpopulation, and few listen or try to do anything about it." In my opinion, we've got to start talking about it if we're going to do anything. And I don't mean talking in a backroom at the Sierra Club or Population Connection. That's preaching to the choir. I mean on CNN, NBC—yes, even on Fox. And I don't mean once a year, but every day!

Imagine that you've just sat down to watch the evening news in February. "The Dow Jones average went up another 50 points today to close at 15,032. The weather forecast is a high of 75, low of 65, and sunny.

"This summary of the national news: Department of Population Secretary Norman Glish announced that India will meet its goal of zero population growth by 2015. This just in: The United Nations has scheduled an international conference on population, with all nations invited."

This, of course, is pure fantasy, but no more so than our suppression of the news by pretending that overpopulation does not exist. Rather, it underlies almost every problem of our time, from global warming to immigration to insufficient water supply.

Appropriate to this is the old Zero Population Growth motto: "No matter what your cause, it's a lost cause if we don't control population."

No, Virginia, the truth is, there is no Santa Claus. He is a fable, but represents the loving kindness of your parents and other grown-ups who take care of you. Yet I know that Santa Claus, if he were real, would want to wish you, and all other American children, and, indeed, all of the children of the world: "Merry Christmas to all. May you have a good life, and a life worth living!"

Malthus: What Did He Say, and Does It Matter?

2011

WHO WAS THOMAS ROBERT MALTHUS? In the mid-nineteenth century, his name was as well known as that of Charles Darwin, whom he preceded by a generation. In fact, Malthus gave stimulus to some of Darwin's ideas about evolution and natural selection. Today, Darwin's name is known to every schoolchild and extolled throughout the scientific world for his revolutionary impact on Western thought. The name of Malthus, on the other hand, is little known, or has been vilified with regard to what he did or didn't say. The world would be vastly better off if we had paid attention to what he did say, and not what we thought he said!

This essay is intended to clarify the Malthus story. The source of most of my information is historian Dr. Gertrude Himmelfarb, who wrote the introduction to a book on Malthus published by Random House in 1960. The book is no longer in print, though Dr. Himmelfarb is still living and writing at this time. A book edited by her was on the front page of the *New York Times Book Review* on January 30, 2011.

Thomas Robert Malthus, familiarly known as Robert, was born in 1766 and died in 1834. His father, Daniel, was an English squire living comfortably in the village of Dorking, England, outside of London. Daniel, active in the intellectual circles of his time, was a supporter of Rousseau and the French Revolution.

Robert was born with the anomalies of harelip and cleft palate and lived out his life with these unfortunate facial and vocal deformities. Because of this, Daniel elected to have him schooled at home by tutors, which undoubtedly contributed to his subsequent demonstrated exceptional intellect and cognition. Robert was admitted to Cambridge University at an early age and was graduated with honors, still in his adolescence. While there, he became a fellow in Jesus College, aspiring to be an Anglican priest; however, maturity led him to realize that this was not a realistic expectation, with his speech defect and facial deformity. He subsequently pursued a degree in mathematics, and in 1805, he was appointed to the first chair of political economy at Haileybury College, remaining there until his death in 1834.

In 1798, at the age of 32, Malthus wrote "An Essay on the Principle of Population, as It Affects the Future Improvement of Society." He was encouraged to do so by his father after a bill was introduced in Parliament, the Poor Law, proposing to proportion relief allowances for poverty to the number of children in a family.

From Malthus's point of view, the proposal was sheer madness. What was intended to alleviate the distress of the poor could only have the effect of aggravating that distress. Population was actually encouraged to increase, without increasing the production of food. From this came his "principle of population," that "the power of population is infinitely greater than the power in the earth to produce subsistence for men." He claimed to have deduced this principle from two sets of postulates: first, that food and sex are both essential to human existence, and second, that while food increases only in arithmetic ratio, population, when unchecked, increases in geometric ratio. He illustrated this with the figures of increasing food supply by 1, 2, 3, 4, 5, 6, 7, 8, 9 ..., while population during the same time interval would be 1, 2, 4, 8, 16, 32, 64, 128, 256 .... What held the population in check, according to Malthus, was the "misery and vice" that lay in wait for those who were imprudent enough to exist on the margin of society, where there were more mouths than loaves, so to speak. The margin of society might be smaller or larger, and misery and vice more or less acute; this would depend on the swing of the historical pendulum between sustenance and reproduction.

Malthus's rather dismal pronouncement came at a time of general euphoria related to the French and American Revolutions and the onset of industrial technology. William Godwin represented the utopian point of view with these words: "There will be no war, no crimes, no administration of justice, as it is called, and no government. Beside this, there will be neither disease, anguish, melancholy, nor resentment. Every man will seek, with ineffable ardor, the good of all."

The Marquis de Condorcet, another utopian, contemplated a future in which man's intellectual and moral perfectibility would be complemented by a physical perfectibility approaching, although not quite achieving, immortality.

Perhaps it is not surprising that the pronouncements of Malthus came as a rude shock to utopians everywhere, including his father, Daniel, who had encouraged him to write it in the first place. Some of his critics developed the misconception that he had the occupation of a practicing minister even though he had abandoned that intention many years before. William Cobet wrote, "Parson, I have, during my life, detested many men, but never anyone so much as you." William Hazlitt vilified the essay as a work "in which the little, low, rankling malice of a parish-beadle is disguised in the garb of philosophy." Other critics referred to "the Parson with eleven daughters who presumed to preach to others the virtues of celibacy."

I should not imply that Robert's essay was met with universal condemnation. It wasn't. His readers tended to be either critics or admirers. In any case, his essay propelled him onto the public stage to a degree far exceeding his temperament. He lived a quiet, scholarly life, was happily married, and had three children, not eleven. His associates all remarked on his exceptional amiability, good nature, and gentleness. He did not seek the limelight.

Robert spent the next five years reading, reflecting, and traveling throughout the world, gathering statistics about population. The second edition of his essay appeared in 1803 and was the basis of all later editions, of which six appeared in Malthus's lifetime and a seventh posthumously.

I now approach the main point of my exposition, that the second treatise, which I label "Malthus II," published in 1803, is fundamentally different from the first, "Malthus I," published in 1798. This is not in regard to his "principle of population," but rather in what could be done about the problem. In Malthus I, he concluded that nothing short of "misery and vice" (war, disease, starvation, and so on) would influence it. Malthus II, in contrast, spoke of "moral restraint."

Quoting Dr. Himmelfarb: "Malthus was moved to compose a second version of the Essay by the mixed reception afforded to the first. On the one hand, the first was far more successful and even influential than the casual circumstances of its publication had led him to expect; on the other hand, it was more bitterly and tellingly attacked than he had anticipated. Inspired as much by the criticism as by the tributes paid him, Malthus addressed himself to the problem of population more seriously than he had done before."

Robert defined moral restraint as "the restraint from marriage which is not followed by irregular gratifications." It is one of the ironies of history that Malthusianism should have come to mean, among other things, the discovery and promotion of mechanical means of birth control. Malthus only referred to chastity.

Moral restraint now occupied first place in Malthus's catalog of preventive checks, taking precedence over misery and vice. He had come a long way from Malthus I, where natural man was a slothful creature and the social order was one that roused him only by applying the most severe and relentless pressures. Most readers of Malthus, however, did not take seriously the revisions of Malthus II, or were even aware of them.

Again, Himmelfarb: "Partly, the fault lies with readers, or non-readers, who find in a book exactly what they expect to find in it. The principle of population was so widely advertised by critics and admirers alike that only a particularly vigilant reader would be aware that something drastic had happened to that principle. And it may be supposed in the case of the Essay, as in any 'classic' of this sort, that more people pretended to read it than did, or at best read it so cursorily as to do no more than to confirm their expectations." Malthusianism was, for them, as it is today, the doctrine that had first attracted attention. In the 1830s and '40s, when his influence was at its height, praise and blame were almost inordinate. The year of his death—1834—was also the year of his greatest triumph. It was then that a new poor law was passed, incorporating his principles and giving relief to the poor not based on family size.

The five-year interval separating the two editions of the essay was spent by Malthus in worldwide travel to study the effect of population on particular societies and nations: primitive people, American Indians, South Sea islanders, Greeks and Romans, and various modern countries (presaging Darwin's subsequent voyages on HMS *Beagle*?). This undoubtedly influenced Robert's viewpoint regarding the future of society.

So what do I conclude? I think Malthus was swindled out of the proper respect he deserved for his incredibly prescient awareness of the inexorable nature of population growth. There was no global overpopulation at the time in which he lived—the earth had about one billion people then. Demographers have estimated that with that number, the world could exist infinitely. But in 2011, the population will soon reach seven billion. No one feels that number can be sustained indefinitely.

I also agree with Dr. Himmelfarb's concluding paragraph: "Most comforting is the doctrine of the later Malthus, the exhortations to moral restraint. For in that Malthus may be found not only the corrective of the excesses of the earlier one, but also a possible corrective of our present situation. Forces that once seemed outside our control—indeed, to Malthus himself once seemed so—were shown to be controllable; and nature itself (including human nature) was shown capable of being tamed and pacified, subjected to our will instead of pursuing a will of its own. It was Malthus' great service not only to diagnose the disease but also to have suggested the cure."

In other words, it is more important to speak of moral restraint (Malthus II), because it gives a glimmer of hope on which one can act, rather than give up in despair on the basis of misery and vice (Malthus I).

Malthus was right, and we should honor his name at least as much as that of Charles Darwin. We live in a time of profound change. You can see it on your television set with the evening news: a sea of humanity in Egypt, Libya, Tunisia, and soon all around the world, demanding a change from autocracy to democracy, from survival of the fittest to survival of the kindest. It will require, too, profound changes in us Americans, who are fortunate enough to live in the land "from sea to shining sea." We must learn to live in what I call "controlled retreat," with cooperation and magnanimity to a degree never before witnessed on the earth. If we fail, and misery and vice prevail, we can say that we tried, as Thomas Robert Malthus did in showing us the way.

"Cool"
2010

My dictionary includes the following definitions for the word *cool*: moderately cold ~ lacking warmth ~ marked by steady dispassionate calmness and self-control ~ lacking ardor or friendliness ~ marked by restrained emotion or excitement ~ marked by deliberate effrontery or lack of due respect or discretion ~ facilitating or suggesting relief from heat ~ of a color with a hue in the range violet through blue to green ~ a casual and nonchalant manner ~ (SLANG) excellent.

I was at the checkout counter at the supermarket. One of the grocery items I had placed in my cart was some bulk candy (chocolate-covered pretzels), with price determined by weight. As the young clerk was weighing the bag, she asked me, "Do you happen to remember how much it is per pound?"

"$2.49," I promptly replied.

"Cool," she said, and rang it up.

As I was driving home, with nothing else to think about, I began to contemplate what she meant by the word *cool*. It occurred to me that there were three deeper and simultaneous meanings.

First, she acknowledged acceptance of my figure, reflecting trust. The price could really have been $2.99 per pound, for example, but she was willing to accept my statement on the face of it. Cool.

Second, "cool" expressed gratitude, since she would have had to send someone to look up the price, with a resultant delay in the line behind me at the counter, a problem averted by my knowledge. Cool.

Third, I detected a fleeting approval, or even admiration, in her voice. I imagined her thinking, "This is the first guy in a week who knew the price of anything." Actually, it was only by chance that I did know it. The prices on the adjacent bins of candy were printed, while that of the chocolate-covered pretzels was handwritten, and it caught my eye. In any case, she seemed impressed. Cool.

Trust, gratitude, admiration—all from one brief utterance, and none of it in the dictionary. Or at least, this is what I imagined she was thinking. It made my day, together with, of course, the chocolate-covered pretzels.

Stories My Father Told Me (I Think) and Selected Short Subjects

2005

FOREWORD

HISTORY IS THE STORY of events now past, and biography is the story of people who made the events happen. Nowhere is there certainty that the "story" is correct—the way it really was. Reassurance is provided by documentation, consultation, and so on, an effort that I have neither time nor reserve to do. I have, therefore, decided not to even try, and I present this story of my family and background solely on the basis of my recollections, realizing that some of the details and my perspective toward the end of my life may not be absolutely accurate. I acknowledge this by using narrative rather than documentary style, and with the hope that it will be more interesting to read.

I write this Manley family history mainly for the awareness of my three children—Ben, Anne, and Bill, who, for whatever reason (likely my own deficiency), had little contact with and perhaps no recollection of the Manleys. Also, of course, for the amusement and bemusement of my dear wife, Kimberly, who will have the task of typing it. Who knows, maybe at some distant time and place it will be of interest to my present grandchildren—Clara, Nell, and Rhys (and later, Parker, born in 2007)—regarding the origin of some of their DNA. In short, it is an FYI.

DAD

DAD WAS BORN on October 25, 1896 on property that is now part of Wilson's Creek Civil War Battlefield National Park, about 15 miles southwest of Springfield, Missouri. He was named Charles Benton Manley, probably after his grandfather Charley B. Manley (1850–1906). The middle name Benton was in honor of Thomas Hart Benton, the flamboyant first U.S. senator from Missouri, who was widely respected among early settlers and was known as "Old Bullion" for his support of the monetary gold standard. Benton fought several duels, including one with Andrew Jackson. There is a statue of him in the U.S. Capitol Building.

Dad was the eldest of eight children of Jesse D. (1875–1946) and Martha Jane Keltner Manley (1873–1949). His siblings' names were Blanche, Birdie (!), Helen, Hazel, Hobart, and Bob, in uncertain order, although Bob was the youngest. We found a marker at the "new" Manley Cemetery (a few miles east of the Wilson's Creek property) indicating another son, Clyde (1908–1918), whom I did not previously know about, likely because he died in childhood.

Apparently, the first of the Manleys at Wilson's Creek were Caleb (1802–1872) and Rebecca (1809–1893). The first English-speaking inland settlers beyond the Mississippi and Missouri Rivers did not arrive until after the Louisiana Purchase in 1803, and more likely after statehood in 1821. A telegraph line was first erected from Arrowrock or Boone's Lick on the Missouri River (west of present-day Boonesville), running southwest to Fort Smith, Arkansas. A road accompanied the telegraph line ("The Old Wire Road") and ran through Springfield and the Wilson's Creek battlefield site, adjacent to Caleb and Rebecca's property.

Genealogical records have established that Caleb and Rebecca were born and married in Fluvanna County, Virginia (between Richmond and Charlottesville) and migrated west to Tennessee, and then Missouri. Thus, they are the original Missouri forebears.

I assume that Charley B. was Caleb and Rebecca's son, although that would have made Rebecca 41 at the time of his birth, not an impossibility. If so, then I am their great-great-grandson. However, there may have been another generation in there. (The monument to Caleb and Rebecca in the "old" Manley Cemetery at Wilson's Creek was placed by a Thomas Manley in 1915.)

When I was growing up, I misunderstood that Dad had been born during the battle (August 10, 1861), with vivid imaginings of cannonballs flying through the windows to add to the drama of the birth scene. Of course, Dad was 35 years too late. It seems clear that Caleb and Rebecca were living there at the time of the battle (aged 59 and 52, respectively), but I am unaware of any information about their experience except that the Confederates (the 3rd Louisiana Volunteers or Weightman's Brigade) had camped on their yard before the battle and likely drank from Manley's Creek, a small tributary running down to Wilson's Creek nearby. I do recall Dad telling me about his maternal grandfather Keltner, who was about 15 at the time and lived someways east of the battlefield. He had heard the boom of cannon in the distance throughout the morning. When the noise later subsided, he walked over to determine its cause. It was a typically hot summer day, and the urgent job of burying the hundreds of dead soldiers fell to the victorious Confederates, the Union army having retreated to Springfield. Great-grandfather Keltner was pressed into service, making him regret his curiosity.

Jesse, Martha, and family moved to another farm on the northwest outskirts of Springfield, probably when Dad was fairly small (in the early 1900s). Jesse started a horse-and-wagon draying (hauling) business and later expanded into the plumbing trade, capitalizing on the new technology of indoor plumbing. By this time, Dad was old enough to help, and he recalled installing plumbing in the new junior high school building where some years later he became principal.

I have the impression that Jesse was successful but never prosperous, likely because of a drinking problem. It's also my understanding that he and Martha later separated but likely never divorced. Jesse died in 1946 just about the time we moved back to Springfield from Tulsa. I never met him, but I recall seeing a newspaper clipping of his obituary.

I do remember Grandmother Manley. I went with Dad several times to visit her; one time, my friend Charles Chalender went along. The farm had been enveloped by the expanding city, but the house was, of course, still an old white frame farmhouse, with a porch on two sides and a large shade tree in front. There were a shed and a reasonably large pasture behind. A new concrete street was being put in out front, and I remember Dad worrying about having to pay for the curbing.

Inside the house, everything sloped: the doorframes, the floors, the narrow staircase to the second floor. I remember worn linoleum and a huge, black, freestanding Franklin-style stove for heat.

Grandmother was quite elderly, frail, and small, and moved about slowly. She also talked slowly, often using, for rhetorical emphasis, "Don't you know?" "Bent (that's what Dad was called)—such and such—don't you know?" I never got to know her very well, but she seemed like a very nice lady. She is buried among other Keltners on the far side of the new Manley Cemetery, well away from the marker for Jesse.

Dad graduated from Central High School in Springfield (as did I), the same school he would return to as principal about 30 years later. When World War I came along, he enlisted and was assigned to the Chemical Warfare Service. He went to Washington, D.C. as a Private First Class and helped make mustard gas, with scars on his forearms to prove it.

Dad was the only one among his siblings who went to college. In those days, it was generally considered a waste of time and something for rich kids to do. I don't know what compelled him, but he would work for a year to save up enough money to go to Drury College in Springfield for a year, then work again, and so forth. One year, he lived in a boarding house in Shawnee, Oklahoma and sold *World Book Encyclopedia* sets to newly rich Indians who had been paid for their land rights. They couldn't read, but they liked to look at the pictures.

Dad told me he used to catch a ride around the Shawnee area in a horse-and-buggy owned by an otherwise propertyless old prospector who lived at the boarding house. On more than one occasion, the old man complained to Dad that no one would pay any attention to his assertion that the sparse and scrubby land they were riding on concealed a large deposit of oil. Unfortunately, Dad didn't pursue it either, as a few years later the Shawnee basin became the largest oil-producing field in the world. Tulsa was known as "the oil capital of the world," and an active oil derrick stood on the grounds of the capitol building in Oklahoma City. I remember as a boy driving between Oklahoma City and Norman, the horizon of that flat land a veritable forest of oil derricks, thousands of them as far as the eye could see.

Later, Dad worked as a roustabout on a derrick and became crew boss despite being younger than some of the other hands. One man expressed his resentment by constant heckling. Finally, Dad took him aside and told him that whether he liked it or not, Dad had been made the boss, and if he didn't like it, they were going to have it out. The heckling stopped. (Perhaps I should explain that Dad was 6 feet 4 inches tall and weighed well over 200 pounds.)

One last oil story. After graduating from Drury College, Dad joined the faculty and taught biology. In his spare time, he became a recruiter for the college to attract prospective students. On one occasion, he traveled to Claremore, Oklahoma to recruit two daughters of a farm family that lived nearby. He was met in the parlor by the mother and the two young applicants, who seemed quite positive toward attending Drury. Dad noted that, for a Sunday afternoon, the father was inappropriately absent, and during their conversation the mother seemed distracted, periodically gazing anxiously out the window. Suddenly, a loud roar commenced, and shortly thereafter the father came running into the house, covered with oil and shouting, "We're rich!" It seems that they had just struck oil on the south forty. The end of the story is that the two daughters were reported to have gone to an East Coast school.

Sounds like a whopper, doesn't it? Well, Dad was a very truthful man, but he liked a good story. I'm telling it the way I remember it.

While attending Drury College, Dad played on the football team as a lineman. (Drury no longer has football, but in those days, they were fairly competitive.) Mom had transferred to Drury from William Woods College, a two-year college for women in Fulton, Missouri. In one game, Dad was injured and carried off the field on a stretcher adjacent to where Mom was standing on the sidelines. That's how they first met! Dad also played first base in what amounted to semi-professional baseball in the local leagues. I remember his baseball glove, which amounted to nothing more than a thin leather glove with no padding or webbing. Later, he was a high school football coach in Joplin, Missouri for a few years. But his best athletic story was when he was a basketball referee.

He and another man used to travel around in a Model T Ford to small towns in southwest Missouri to referee high school basketball games. Many towns were very isolated in those days before radio and television, and most of the roads were dirt and occasionally necessitated fording a stream. I can see them in their Model T heading out through the countryside in their black-and-white uniforms, with spare basketballs in the back seat. One evening, they traveled to an isolated backwoods town (I don't remember the name) that was known to have a good basketball team, particularly when they played at home. In fact, they had never lost at home!

The "gym" occupied the second floor of an old feed store. The court required the full length of the building so that the baskets and backboards were affixed to the brick walls at either end. Some room was available on one side for bleachers, which were filled to capacity with the partisan local crowd.

The whistle blew, the ball was thrown, and the game began. Before long, a local player made a breakaway and as he approached the basket, he leaped up and slam dunked the ball through the hoop. The only problem was that in order to aid his leap, he had inserted his foot in a chink due to a conveniently missing brick halfway up to the basket. They must have practiced for hours to develop this technique of assisted slam dunk, presaging by many years the unassisted variety of today.

The crowd roared approval, but Dad whistled the ball dead. "Illegal move. Basket canceled. You can't do that." Well, it was a long night, ending in the first loss ever at home for the local team. It's my understanding that Dad and his co-conspirator had to sneak out of town and never went back.

MOM

Mom was born on April 1, 1898 in Madelia, Minnesota, which I've never seen but understand to be a wide spot in the road in the south-central part of the state, 25 miles west of Mankato. She was named Edna Harriett Ewers (pronounced "yours"). (Years later in St. Louis, their next-door neighbor was a Mrs. Mine: "How do you do, Mrs. Ewers?" "How do you do, Mrs. Mine?")

There are extensive genealogy files for the Ewers, who are traced all the way back to Flanders at the time of Charlemagne, then to England, and much later to America. Through generations, they gradually worked their way across to Iowa. Both of Mom's parents were born and raised in Albia, Iowa, a town of about 4,000 people in south-central Iowa. Grandfather's name was Albert Francis Ewers, and Grandmother's name was Mildred Hickenlouper. She was a cousin to Henry A. Wallace, vice president with F.D.R. and later Progressive Party candidate for president.

Shortly after Mom was born, the family moved to St. Louis, where she grew up at 3411A Pestalozzi Street in south St. Louis. A century later, it remains essentially unchanged—a two-story, red-brick duplex, like all the rest of the homes on the street. (As Tennessee Williams recalled, St. Louis houses all have the color of old mustard or dried blood.) Uncle Bob, Mom's younger brother who lived downstairs, used to say that the Busch family lived at one end of Pestalozzi and they lived at the other. (The east end of the street runs into the Anheuser-Busch brewery, where Adolphus Busch originally lived.) Our family visited there when I was a small boy, driving up from Tulsa, a trip that took several days. The thing I remember most about their house was an old iron nutcracker, in the shape of a squirrel, that was used as a doorstop. The nut was cracked in the squirrel's mouth by cranking the tail. I always checked it out first when we went to visit.

Grandfather Ewers was a principal and taught at Roosevelt High School in St. Louis. He also owned a well-known girl's summer camp near Hackensack, in upper/mid-Minnesota on Leach Lake, from the 1920s until his death in 1946. I remember as a child in Tulsa being envious that my sisters got to spend several summers at the camp in Minnesota while I stayed in sweltering Oklahoma.

Grandfather also had a strong interest in botany, and I understand that at least one species of plant is named after him (Ewersiana?), although I have not been able to prove it. He died about the end of World War II, I think of heart disease.

Grandmother Ewers, who lived to be about 95, was short and petite, like Mom. (Mother was less than 5 feet tall and weighed less than 100 pounds; she and Dad were a real Mutt-and-Jeff couple.) Mom had two younger brothers: Al, who grew up to run a stationery store in Louisville, Kentucky—his wife was Louise—and Bob, who with his wife, Martha, and many children lived in the lower part of the duplex on Pestalozzi. Uncle Bob had a clerical job at the Missouri State Unemployment Office. Both he and Martha smoked heavily and died in middle age as a result.

I know almost nothing about Mom's childhood, except I remember her saying that she used to ride the trolley out to Forest Park, at the edge of the city. After she graduated from high school, she got a job, without her father's permission, working at a flower shop. That lasted about two weeks, when Grandfather found out about it and made her quit. He felt that no respectable woman worked. She collected her paycheck and bought a new hat with the money. That was the only job she ever had.

She then went to William Woods College in Fulton. One night, there was a fair in town. She and her roommate wanted to go, but there was a curfew. Somehow, they got some boy's clothes and snuck out to the fair in disguise. On the way home, they spied a policeman walking his beat. To escape detection, they each grabbed a stick and ran it along a picket fence as they skipped down the sidewalk, just like boys might do. It worked. Straight out of *Tom Sawyer*.

After William Woods, Mom transferred to Drury College in Springfield, where she met Dad.

US

DAD AND MOM GRADUATED from Drury College in 1921 and got married the same year, on December 28. While teaching biology at Drury, he was a member of the first spelunking team to explore Marvel Cave (now part of Silver Dollar City near Branson) and to identify the underground animal life. Dad attended graduate school during the summers, and over many years' time he obtained master's and doctorate degrees in education from Columbia University in New

This 1945 portrait of my father, Charles Benton Manley, Sr. has hung in my home for many years. As principal of high schools in Tulsa, Oklahoma and Springfield, Missouri, he was the source of inspiration to many people there—including to me, as a sort of Atticus Finch. The portrait was painted by Charles Kubilos, then a senior at Will Rogers High School in Tulsa.

York City, finishing in about 1938. Along the way, he became principal at Pipkin Junior High School in Springfield, where he had helped install the plumbing with his dad. For a time, he was football coach at Joplin (Missouri) High School.

Patty and Marge were born in Springfield, Patty on November 2, 1926 and Marge on November 9, 1930. The family moved to Tulsa, Oklahoma, where Dad became principal at Horace Mann Junior High School. About 1940, he became principal at the new Will Rogers High School on the outskirts of the city. It was a showcase high school at the time, and educators came from all over to see it.

I was born on June 12, 1933 in Tulsa. In 1946, after World War II had ended, we moved back to Springfield, where Dad became principal of the senior high school. Patty had gone on to the University of Oklahoma in Norman. Dad had an "understanding" that he would later replace the existing superintendent of schools (a Mr. Study) when he retired. Although Dad was widely respected throughout the school system, a local politician maneuvered into the job when it became available in the early 1950s. Dad became assistant superintendent of schools and did the superintendent's job without the credit. I remember the folks being very upset when he didn't get the job, and they left town for a few days to avoid the local press. As usual, we didn't talk about it, but I was very angry at this man and plotted what I could do to get even (but, of course, never did).

Dad retired about 1961, then taught part-time at Evangel College (an Assembly of God college) in Springfield. After a number of years of suffering from angina pectoris, he died while shaving one morning from a heart attack at age 70 (February 12, 1967).

Dad was a quiet, reserved, imposing, and handsome man who exuded authority without having to assert it. This was particularly true at school, which was, in part, what made him such a good principal. I can remember when growing up in Tulsa that my neighborhood playmates never wanted to enter my house for fear of encountering him. In later years, he wore half–reading glasses and had a way of tilting his head forward quite innocently to peer over the top of them to see who was there, this visage being sufficient to send any child scurrying. Understand that he was not *their* principal, but they knew he was *a* principal.

I grew up being often identified as "the principal's son" and did my best to conceal the fact, particularly later in Springfield when I went to the only high school and he was the principal. The school was across town, so we drove together in the morning, but we had an understanding that he would let me out at the corner so as to enter the building separately. By this means, and since there were other Manleys in town, I generally succeeded in getting through high school with only my closest friends knowing that "he" was my father, and that any grades or achievements that I attained were not through any special privilege or connections, thereby avoiding the sure-to-be razzing.

At home, although reserved by nature, Dad was, in fact, a kindly, gentle man and Mom generally "ruled the roost." His favorite pastime was to be out in the garage working on the family car, a 1937 Pontiac sedan. In those Depression/War years, this maintenance was almost a necessity with one working parent on a schoolteacher's salary. I drove it off to college in 1951, and it lasted several years of my handling after that: 150,000 miles and, I'm sure, it never saw the inside of an auto repair shop. It was big, it was long, it was high, and it was made entirely of steel. It was like a tank. We called it "the Green Monster." A modern car would encounter it like an aluminum can meeting an anvil. Long, sloping front fenders, side running boards, a vertical trunk. The gear shift stuck out of the floor about a meter long with a black knob on the end. Shifting it was like driving some mysterious Eastern religion.

Dad coaxed it through the years with his loving hands. I was fortunate to witness the final reboring of the cylinders in the massive iron block of an engine, such that only racing pistons would fit the longer holes, but assuring that the Green Monster would end its time in style.

Dad was always on the lookout for stray nuts, bolts, screws, and nails lying on the sidewalk, curb, street, or counter; he would harvest them and place them in one of several metal cans, to be opened later in time of need and spread on a greasy rag until just the proper item was found. After his death, I found these cans again, still waiting expectantly to serve. They should have been buried with him, but as it is, I don't remember what happened to them. They were probably thrown out.

On Saturday nights, Dad was usually found sitting in a comfortable wingback living room chair, preparing his adult Sunday School lesson for the following morning at the Central Avenue Christian Church (Disciples of Christ). Occasionally, he and Mom would go to the downtown movies with free tickets provided by the theater to the Board of Education. Weeknights in later years, they might exchange with Judge and Mrs. Chalender to watch *Gunsmoke* or *I Love Lucy* over TV tables.

Mom, though not verbose, was more talkative than Dad. She subordinated herself completely to her role as wife, mother, and homemaker and excelled at all three. I know of no other hobbies or interests that she had; homemaking was her full-time job. She never drove a car until Dad died, then promptly did so as if she'd driven all her life. As far as I recall, she rarely left the house except with Dad or to go shopping. She had no outside interests, organizations, or friends. She always wore housedresses and stockings, with an apron in the kitchen. We had three complete meals a day, every day, with dessert after both lunch and dinner. Breakfast began with juice or fruit, according to the season, then cereal, leading up to eggs and bacon or ham with toast. There was always meat for dinner, such as pork chops or steak. The cookie jar was always full of homemade cookies, often of more than one variety, but I remember "refrigerator" cookies most. (A log of dough was wrapped in a damp towel and kept in the refrigerator, slices being cut off and baked as needed.) The house was always neat and orderly and the beds made, and Mom was always busy doing something, like washing dishes. It was like a fantastic B&B—only we got lunch and dinner, too. In the basement, she had an electric washing machine with an attached wringer, and she hung all the clothes out to dry. I never recall her sitting down except in the evening to read a magazine or book, or when they finally got a TV—one of the last in our neighborhood. Mom was always even-tempered, and I never recall my parents having a fight or even raising their voices. They were completely devoted to each other, and I assumed the whole world was that way.

My earliest memory was throwing my baby bottle out the open apartment window in New York City; my mother said, "Well, that's the end of that." On my fifth birthday, toward the end of our last full year in New York, my father took me to buy a new pair of shoes. When I arrived home, quite proud, my sisters pronounced them "girl's shoes"—another traumatic imprint leading to an immediate return to the store for exchange.

I started kindergarten in Tulsa in the fall of 1938 with Miss White at Barnard Grade School ("Barnyard"). We had returned to a different house several blocks away and with an address forever engraved on my memory: 1836 East 15th Street. There, my childhood occurred, the center of the earth, during the next eight years (it seemed like at least 50), until we moved back to Springfield in 1946.

Fifteenth Street was quite wide and would have been busy except for gas rationing. Even so, it separated two worlds. Our house was a neat, small, five-room white frame bungalow appropriate to the lower (but respectable) middle class of a school official and similar to all its neighbors (pawns), while each house across the street was multi-floored, elevated, distinctive, and imposing (pieces). One estate had

My first bike.

a brick wall and gate, another was "Tara" (a white-columned Southern classic). One had a swimming pool, another a tennis court. All of the garages on both sides of the street were separate and at the rear of the property. On the back of each garage was a small, single room and bathroom, intended for the maid, even for the lower middle class. We never had a maid, so we used ours as a clubhouse for kids' activities.

My sisters, Marge and Patty, and I.

    Patty, six and a half years older than I, resembled our mother: short, petite, and pretty. I remember boys calling and hanging around the house during her high school years. Patty graduated in Tulsa and went on to the University of Oklahoma, where she met Larney coming back from the war. They married, he became a geologist, and they headed southwest to the Permian Basin for a life in Midland, Texas, with family, golf, and oil drilling, superlative at all three.

Marge, two and a half years older than I, was tall, quiet, and the smartest of us three. She became a mathematician, married a professor of economics at Iowa State University, and had four children.

The Second World War, to me, consisted of maps of North Africa or Europe on the front page of the *Tulsa Daily World*, with large white arrows showing the positions and movements of the Allies (the United States and Britain) and black arrows for the Axis (Germany and Italy). Otherwise, it meant no chocolate; rationing of gas, sugar, and soda pop (waiting in line at the neighborhood drugstore once a week with six empties); and frequent war drives for various materials needed for the war effort: scrap metal, waste fat, and—oh yes—coat hangers. Ten coat hangers were the necessary admission price to our neighborhood Delman Theatre, three to four blocks away, on Saturday afternoon to see the latest war movie. This provided the stimulus for my buddies and me to go door to door, appearing at our patriotic and angelic best, to beg for coat hangers. Once entry to the theater was gained (as my wife, Kimberly, has heard before), our routine was to sit through the movie once, then during the second showing to "play." This was a form of hide-and-seek in the dark, with us hiding and the ushers seeking. I swear that I recall seeing my friend Dick Drane streak across the lip of the stage with the usher right behind him, their shadows projected on the movie screen.

SUMMING UP

THIS SAMPLING OF ANECDOTES from the Manley family history is intended to provide an admittedly tenuous continuity between the genealogical charts and my own recall. But it's got to end someplace. This is provided by a confluence of three epochal events in my life: (1) the end of World War II, (2) our move back to Missouri, and (3) my advance into adolescence. By June 1946, the war was clearly over and the "Cold War" had clearly begun (Stalin's throwing down the gauntlet, followed by Churchill's "Iron Curtain" speech at Westminster College in Fulton—both in March 1946). Meanwhile, the new Broadway musical hit *Oklahoma* was spotlighting a generally unknown part of the world that I had assumed was its center and that was now receding forever in the rearview mirror. Simultaneously, I was rapidly changing from a skinny but otherwise adequately proportioned little boy (I was first-string halfback on my organized grade school football team) into a tall, nearly emaciated teenager. Dad thought I had polio.

Ahead lay a new state, town, and life (eighth grade), little of which needs emphasis except for my friendship with Charles Chalender, the best friend of my life. I'm sure he will agree that this mainly came about because of his dear mother, Eural ("Mom Chalender"), who threatened him within an inch of his life, to walk the one and a half blocks or so, step onto our porch, ring the bell, introduce himself, and welcome us to Springfield. I'm sure I would never have been able to do it, but he did. Thus began many years of friendship.

Much of the time was spent sitting around their kitchen table, with Mom Chalender trying to get me to eat. That should have been easy, as she was an outstanding cook, like my mother. Regardless, I don't think I gained an ounce. Judge Chalender personified what I thought a judge should look and act like, and I conducted myself accordingly.

And so we progressed from bikes and scouts to cars and girls. ("That Mary Ellen Blaine is a nice girl. Why don't you ask her out?") We had many great times before heading off to the University of Missouri.

Back to June 1946. It was nighttime before we crossed the state line into Missouri. Driving through the first town we came to—there were no express highways in those days—we passed a cocktail lounge with a neon sign in the window that spelled a word I had never seen before: "LIQUOR." I asked, "What was that?" This was the final confirmation that my new life had begun.

ADDEN-DUMB

ADDENDUM, -DENDA. I looked it up in the dictionary. It means "additions that can be made as corrections to anecdotal biographies, that had been intended but forgotten" (literally, from the Latin, "dumb, an den some").

These two classic stories, one relating to my sisters while growing up in Tulsa, and the other to Charles Chalender in Springfield, can simply be added as addenda to the previous material. Both are intended to add a bit of weight, in the tradition of "stories my father told me."

As in any normal sibling relationship, I would periodically get into altercations (fights) with my sisters (Marge, primarily, being next older in age). Although fairly evenly matched (her age by my aggression), she often got in the first blow. The ensuing commotion would bring Mother to the scene just as I was about to deliver a retaliatory strike. She naturally assumed that I had already done so and was, in fact, the perpetrator of the difficulties in the first place, and would immediately put a halt to any further aggression. Stung by the injustice of it all, I once uttered the memorable line, "Aw, Ma, let me hit her just once, Ma, just once."

I RECENTLY RECEIVED AN E-MAIL from Charles Chalender, with the number 52-873 following his name. The explanation for this seemingly arcane—but to me, immediately understood—identification provides the basis for the other memory of growing up that I want to preserve.

The year was 1948 or so. On a lazy summer afternoon, Chalender and I were sitting on the back porch steps of my house watching the auto traffic go by on Grand Avenue. Although automobile production had resumed and increased since the end of the war, cars were still a small fraction of their presence today, so this was a not uncommon way of wasting time.

Our only problem with this non-activity was a car parked at the curb, partially obstructing our view of the street. I hadn't seen it there before. Cars were not ordinarily parked on streets in those days, particularly in our neighborhood. It represented an intrusion. We began speculating, à la the Hardy Boys, as to its significance. The longer we and the car sat there, the more ominous and foreboding it became. Surely, whoever owned that car was up to no good, and it was our responsibility to establish that fact.

As time passed and no driver appeared, however, our sense of duty gradually diminished. Finally, we absolved the termination of our watch by noting the license plate number of the car (no letters in those days), to be promptly reported following any incident in our neighborhood. Having no writing materials at hand, we agreed to check one another's memory of the number on a periodic basis, and we have continued to do so over the subsequent 57 years, especially on birthdays and holidays, and in occasional encounters and written communication. We are happy to certify that our recall remains intact, and that there has yet to be reported any untoward incident in the neighborhood. 52-873.

Dogged Doggerel
AND OTHER
LITERARY DIVERSIONS

was designed by Daniel Franklin and composed by
Village Bookworks, Inc. of Belleville, Illinois, in the typeface Arno.
Robert Slimbach based his design of Arno on the
calligraphically inspired humanistic types of the Italian Renaissance
and named the typeface for the Arno River, which flows
through Florence, the center of the Renaissance.